Mastering Software Engineering: A Comprehensive Guide for Engineers

Jaime Bob

Copyright © [2023]

Title: Mastering Software Engineering: A Comprehensive Guide for Engineers

Author's: Jaime Bob

All rights reserved. No part of this publication may be reproduced, stored in a retrieval system, or transmitted in any form or by any means, electronic, mechanical, photocopying, recording, or otherwise, without the prior written permission of the publisher or author, except in the case of brief quotations embodied in critical reviews and certain other non-commercial uses permitted by copyright law.

This book was printed and published by [Publisher's: **Jaime Bob**] in [2023]

TABLE OF CONTENT

Chapter 1: Introduction to Software Engineering   07

Overview of Software Engineering

Importance of Software Engineering in the Engineering Field

Evolution of Software Engineering

Chapter 2: Software Development Life Cycle   13

Waterfall Model

Agile Methodology

Iterative and Incremental Development

Comparison of Different SDLC Models

Chapter 3: Requirements Engineering   22

Gathering and Eliciting Requirements

Requirements Analysis and Documentation

Validation and Verification of Requirements

Chapter 4: Software Design Principles   28

Object-Oriented Design

Design Patterns

Architectural Design

Component-Based Design

Chapter 5: Software Development Tools and Technologies   36

Integrated Development Environments (IDEs)

Version Control Systems

Test Automation Tools

Collaboration and Project Management Tools

Chapter 6: Software Testing and Quality Assurance   44

Testing Techniques and Strategies

Test Planning and Execution

Defect Tracking and Management

Continuous Integration and Continuous Delivery (CI/CD)

Chapter 7: Software Maintenance and Evolution　　　52

Software Maintenance Processes

Enhancement and Modification of Existing Software

Legacy System Modernization

Software Retirement and Decommissioning

Chapter 8: Software Project Management　　　61

Project Planning and Estimation

Resource Allocation and Management

Risk Management

Agile Project Management

Chapter 9: Software Engineering Ethics and Professionalism　　　69

Ethical Dilemmas in Software Engineering

Responsibility towards Clients and Users

Intellectual Property Rights

Professional Development and Continuing Education

Chapter 10: Emerging Trends in Software Engineering   77

Artificial Intelligence and Machine Learning in Software Engineering

Internet of Things (IoT) and Software Engineering

DevOps and Continuous Deployment

Blockchain Technology for Software Engineering

Chapter 11: Case Studies in Software Engineering   85

Real-life Examples of Successful Software Engineering Projects

Lessons Learned from Failed Software Projects

Best Practices and Success Factors in Software Engineering

Chapter 12: Conclusion   92

Recap of Key Concepts

Future Directions in Software Engineering

Final Thoughts and Recommendations for Engineers

Chapter 1: Introduction to Software Engineering

Overview of Software Engineering

Software engineering is a rapidly evolving field within the realm of information technology. It encompasses the systematic development, operation, and maintenance of software systems, aiming to create reliable and efficient solutions to complex problems. This subchapter provides engineers in the information technology industry with a comprehensive overview of software engineering, highlighting its key concepts, principles, and methodologies.

The chapter begins by defining software engineering and its significance in the modern world. It emphasizes the importance of software in various industries, from healthcare and finance to transportation and entertainment. Software engineering plays a critical role in developing robust, secure, and scalable solutions that meet the specific needs and requirements of businesses and end-users.

Next, the subchapter explores the fundamental principles of software engineering. It delves into the software development life cycle, highlighting its different phases such as requirements gathering, analysis, design, implementation, testing, deployment, and maintenance. The chapter emphasizes the need for a systematic and iterative approach to software development, emphasizing the importance of collaboration, communication, and documentation throughout the process.

Furthermore, the subchapter discusses various software engineering methodologies, including traditional waterfall, agile, and DevOps. It explains the strengths and weaknesses of each approach, helping engineers understand which methodology is best suited for their projects. It also introduces popular software development frameworks such as Scrum and Kanban, providing engineers with practical insights into managing and organizing their development teams.

The subchapter also covers essential software engineering concepts such as software quality assurance, software testing, and software configuration management. It explains the importance of these concepts in ensuring the reliability, performance, and security of software systems. It also introduces engineers to various testing techniques and tools that aid in validating software functionality and identifying potential issues.

To conclude, this subchapter provides engineers in the information technology industry with a comprehensive overview of software engineering. It equips them with the necessary knowledge and understanding of the key concepts, principles, and methodologies in software engineering, enabling them to develop high-quality, scalable, and efficient software solutions. By mastering software engineering, engineers can contribute towards the growth and success of their organizations in an increasingly digital world.

Importance of Software Engineering in the Engineering Field

In today's rapidly evolving technological landscape, it is impossible to ignore the crucial role that software engineering plays in the engineering field, particularly in the niche of information technology. Software engineering has become an essential component of any engineering project, as it enables engineers to design, develop, and maintain complex software systems that drive innovation and efficiency.

One of the key reasons why software engineering is of utmost importance in the engineering field is its ability to streamline and automate processes. Engineers rely heavily on software applications to optimize their workflows, enhance productivity, and perform complex calculations. By utilizing software engineering principles, engineers can develop custom software solutions tailored to their specific needs, allowing them to tackle intricate engineering problems with ease.

Moreover, software engineering plays a central role in ensuring the reliability and safety of engineering projects. In fields such as civil engineering, where the construction of bridges, buildings, and infrastructure is involved, software engineering allows engineers to simulate and analyze various scenarios before the actual construction takes place. This helps identify potential flaws or weaknesses in the design, enabling engineers to make necessary adjustments and ensure the safety and integrity of the final product.

Furthermore, software engineering enables engineers to harness the power of data. In the era of big data, engineers are required to process and analyze vast amounts of information to derive meaningful insights. By applying software engineering principles, engineers can develop sophisticated data processing algorithms and tools that facilitate data-driven decision-making. This not only enhances the accuracy and efficiency of engineering projects but also enables engineers to uncover hidden patterns and trends that can lead to innovative solutions.

Additionally, software engineering enables collaboration and communication among engineering teams. In today's interconnected world, engineers often work in global teams spread across different locations. Software engineering provides engineers with the necessary tools and frameworks to collaborate effectively, share information, and work seamlessly together. From version control systems to project management tools, software engineering facilitates efficient teamwork, ensuring that engineering projects are completed on time and within budget.

In conclusion, software engineering is of paramount importance in the engineering field, especially in the niche of information technology. From streamlining processes and ensuring safety to harnessing the power of data and enabling collaboration, software engineering empowers engineers to drive innovation, efficiency, and excellence in their endeavors. As the engineering field continues to evolve, mastering software engineering is becoming increasingly critical for engineers to stay competitive and deliver exceptional results.

Evolution of Software Engineering

In the rapidly evolving world of Information Technology, the field of software engineering has seen significant advancements and transformations. This subchapter explores the fascinating journey of software engineering, highlighting key milestones and developments that have shaped the discipline into what it is today.

The origins of software engineering can be traced back to the 1950s, when the first computers were developed. At that time, programming was a relatively new concept, and software development was an ad hoc process without any established methodologies or best practices. Engineers relied heavily on trial and error, often resulting in time-consuming and error-prone code.

As computer systems grew in complexity and organizations became increasingly reliant on software, the need for a more structured approach to software development emerged. This led to the birth of software engineering as a formal discipline in the 1960s. Engineers recognized the importance of applying engineering principles to software development, including systematic requirements analysis, design, coding, testing, and maintenance.

The 1970s marked a significant milestone with the advent of structured programming techniques. Engineers began using structured programming languages, such as Pascal and C, which allowed for modular design and improved code readability. This approach helped reduce errors and made software development more efficient.

In the 1980s, the field of software engineering witnessed the rise of object-oriented programming (OOP). OOP revolutionized software development by introducing concepts like encapsulation, inheritance, and polymorphism. This paradigm shift enabled engineers to build more modular, reusable, and maintainable software systems.

The 1990s brought about the widespread adoption of software development process models, such as the waterfall model, iterative models, and agile methodologies. These process models aimed to address the challenges of managing software projects, ensuring higher quality, and meeting customer expectations. Agile methodologies, in particular, emphasized collaboration, adaptability, and rapid delivery, enabling engineers to respond to changing requirements more effectively.

In recent years, software engineering has seen further advancements driven by emerging technologies like artificial intelligence, machine learning, and cloud computing. These technologies have opened up new possibilities for software development, enabling engineers to build intelligent systems, leverage big data, and deliver scalable applications.

As software engineering continues to evolve, engineers must stay updated with the latest trends and advancements in the field. This subchapter provides a glimpse into the remarkable journey of software engineering, highlighting the key milestones and developments that have shaped the discipline. By understanding the evolution of software engineering, engineers can gain valuable insights into the past, present, and future of this dynamic field, empowering them to become more effective and innovative practitioners.

Chapter 2: Software Development Life Cycle

Waterfall Model

In the world of software engineering, the Waterfall Model is one of the most widely recognized and oldest project management methodologies. It is a sequential design process that follows a linear and rigid approach, where each phase of development is completed before moving on to the next. This subchapter will delve into the details of the Waterfall Model, its advantages, disadvantages, and the appropriate scenarios for its implementation.

The Waterfall Model consists of several distinct phases, including requirements gathering, system design, implementation, testing, deployment, and maintenance. Each phase is carefully planned and executed in a sequential manner, with little to no overlap between them. This makes it an ideal choice for projects with well-defined and stable requirements, where changes are expected to be minimal throughout the development process.

One of the major advantages of the Waterfall Model is its simplicity. Its linear nature allows for easy documentation and clear communication between different stakeholders. Engineers can better estimate the time and resources required for each phase, enabling efficient planning and budgeting. Additionally, the Waterfall Model provides a clear structure for project management, making it easier to track progress and ensure that deadlines are met.

However, the Waterfall Model does have its limitations. Its rigidity can be a disadvantage in situations where requirements are likely to change or evolve over time. Once a phase is completed, it becomes challenging to make modifications without going back to the initial stages, leading to potential delays and increased costs. Furthermore, the lack of customer involvement until the final implementation phase may result in a product that does not fully meet the end-user's expectations.

The Waterfall Model is particularly well-suited for large-scale projects in the field of Information Technology. It is commonly employed in the development of enterprise-level software systems, where requirements are typically stable and well-defined. Engineers working on such projects can benefit from the methodology's systematic and disciplined approach, ensuring a high level of quality and predictability in the final product.

In conclusion, the Waterfall Model remains a valuable methodology in the field of software engineering, especially for projects with clear and stable requirements. Understanding its advantages and disadvantages is crucial for engineers in the Information Technology niche, as it allows them to make informed decisions regarding the best approach to project management. By mastering the Waterfall Model, engineers can enhance their ability to successfully deliver high-quality software solutions.

Agile Methodology

In the rapidly evolving field of Information Technology, it is crucial for engineers to adopt software development methodologies that enable flexibility, adaptability, and speed. Agile methodology has emerged as a proven approach that allows engineers to effectively navigate complex projects, meet customer requirements, and deliver high-quality software solutions.

Agile methodology is a collaborative and iterative approach to software development, emphasizing frequent communication, continuous improvement, and rapid delivery. It promotes a mindset shift from traditional, linear development processes towards a more dynamic and customer-centric approach. Unlike traditional methodologies such as Waterfall, which follow a sequential process, Agile methodology embraces change and encourages engineers to adapt to evolving customer needs and project requirements.

One of the key principles of Agile methodology is the concept of self-organizing, cross-functional teams. Engineers from different disciplines, such as software development, quality assurance, and user experience, collaborate closely throughout the entire development lifecycle. This fosters effective communication, knowledge sharing, and a sense of ownership among team members, resulting in quicker problem-solving and improved decision-making.

Another crucial aspect of Agile methodology is the use of short development cycles called sprints. Sprints typically last two to four weeks and involve a set of prioritized user stories or requirements. Engineers work together to design, develop, test, and deliver a working increment of the software at the end of each sprint. This iterative process allows for frequent feedback from stakeholders, early identification of issues, and the ability to quickly adapt and adjust project direction.

Continuous integration and continuous delivery (CI/CD) are integral components of Agile methodology. CI/CD practices ensure that software changes are frequently integrated into a shared repository and automatically tested, allowing for early bug detection and smoother integration. This enables engineers to deliver software to customers faster, reducing time-to-market and increasing customer satisfaction.

To successfully implement Agile methodology, engineers must embrace key values such as transparency, collaboration, and adaptability. Communication channels should be open and transparent, fostering a culture of trust and knowledge sharing. Regular meetings, such as daily stand-ups and sprint planning sessions, are essential to keep the entire team aligned and focused on project goals.

In conclusion, Agile methodology has revolutionized the field of software engineering by providing a flexible, customer-centric approach to development. By embracing Agile practices, engineers in the Information Technology industry can effectively manage complex projects, deliver high-quality software solutions, and meet ever-changing customer requirements.

Iterative and Incremental Development

In the fast-paced world of Information Technology, software engineering plays a pivotal role in creating robust and efficient systems. One of the most effective approaches to software development is iterative and incremental development. This subchapter aims to introduce engineers to this method and help them understand its significance in the field.

Iterative and incremental development is a software development methodology that focuses on creating software in small, manageable increments, with each iteration building upon the previous one. This approach allows for flexibility, adaptability, and continuous improvement throughout the development process.

One of the main advantages of iterative and incremental development is its ability to deliver value early in the development cycle. Instead of waiting for the complete system to be developed, engineers can deliver a working product in smaller iterations. This allows for quicker feedback from stakeholders and end-users, enabling the team to make necessary adjustments and improvements along the way.

Another benefit of this approach is its ability to manage risks effectively. By breaking down the development process into smaller iterations, engineers can identify and address potential issues early on. This mitigates the risk of costly mistakes and allows for better risk management throughout the project.

Furthermore, iterative and incremental development promotes collaboration and continuous learning. By involving stakeholders and end-users in each iteration, engineers can gather valuable feedback and insights. This feedback can then be used to improve subsequent iterations, ensuring that the final product meets the needs and expectations of the users.

To implement iterative and incremental development successfully, engineers need to adopt certain practices and principles. These include regular communication and collaboration among team members, continuous integration and testing, and the use of agile project management methodologies.

In conclusion, iterative and incremental development is a powerful approach in the field of software engineering, particularly in Information Technology. By breaking down the development process into smaller iterations, engineers can deliver value early, manage risks effectively, and promote collaboration and continuous learning. By understanding and implementing this methodology, engineers can enhance their software development practices and deliver high-quality systems to their users and stakeholders.

Comparison of Different SDLC Models

Introduction

In the field of software engineering, the Software Development Life Cycle (SDLC) is a crucial framework that guides the development process of software systems. It provides a structured approach to ensure efficient and effective software development, from the initial concept to the final deployment. There are several SDLC models available, each with its own advantages and disadvantages. This subchapter aims to provide a comprehensive comparison of different SDLC models, enabling engineers in the information technology niche to make informed decisions based on specific project requirements.

Waterfall Model

The Waterfall model is the most traditional and sequential SDLC model. It follows a linear approach, where each phase is completed before moving on to the next. This model is best suited for projects with well-defined requirements and stable environments. Its advantages include simplicity, clear documentation, and ease of project management. However, it lacks flexibility, as changes in requirements during later stages can be challenging to accommodate.

Agile Model

The Agile model is an iterative and incremental SDLC model that promotes collaboration, flexibility, and adaptability. It focuses on delivering working software in short iterations, allowing for continuous feedback and improvement. Agile is ideal for projects with evolving requirements and dynamic environments. Its benefits include increased customer satisfaction, early and frequent deliveries, and improved team communication. However, it requires active customer involvement and may not be suitable for large-scale projects with fixed deadlines.

Spiral Model

The Spiral model combines elements of both the Waterfall and Agile models. It emphasizes risk analysis and mitigation through multiple iterations. Each iteration includes planning, designing, building, and testing phases. This model is suitable for large and complex projects, where the cost of failure is high. Its advantages include risk reduction, early software prototypes, and flexibility in accommodating changes. However, it requires experienced personnel and can be time-consuming and costly.

Incremental Model

The Incremental model breaks down the software development process into smaller modules, which are developed and delivered incrementally. It allows for early and partial system functionality and facilitates easier testing and integration. This model is suitable for projects with multiple stakeholders and evolving requirements. Its benefits include early customer feedback, reduced development time, and improved risk management. However, it requires careful planning and coordination among different development teams.

Conclusion

Choosing the right SDLC model is crucial for successful software development projects. The Waterfall model suits well-defined and stable environments, while the Agile model is ideal for dynamic and evolving requirements. The Spiral model emphasizes risk analysis and mitigation, while the Incremental model allows for early and partial system functionality. Engineers in the information technology niche should carefully consider project requirements and constraints when selecting an appropriate SDLC model. By understanding the advantages and disadvantages of each model, they can ensure efficient software development and ultimately deliver high-quality solutions to their clients.

Chapter 3: Requirements Engineering

Gathering and Eliciting Requirements

In the world of software engineering, the success of a project heavily relies on the initial phase of gathering and eliciting requirements. This crucial step sets the foundation for the entire development process and ensures that the final product meets the needs and expectations of the end-users. In this subchapter, we will delve into the importance of requirements gathering and provide engineers in the field of Information Technology with a comprehensive guide to mastering this critical phase.

The process of gathering and eliciting requirements begins with effective communication between engineers and stakeholders. Engineers must actively engage with stakeholders to understand their needs, preferences, and constraints. This involves conducting interviews, surveys, and workshops to gain a holistic understanding of the project's objectives. By establishing clear lines of communication, engineers can ensure that all parties involved are aligned from the start.

Once requirements have been gathered, engineers must elicit the necessary information to validate and refine these requirements. This involves asking probing questions, analyzing existing systems, and conducting feasibility studies. By eliciting further details, engineers can identify potential gaps or inconsistencies in the requirements, helping to uncover hidden needs that may have been overlooked initially.

In this subchapter, we will explore various techniques for gathering and eliciting requirements. We will discuss the importance of active listening, as it allows engineers to truly understand the stakeholders' needs and concerns. Additionally, we will introduce the concept of requirements documentation and explain how engineers can effectively capture and organize requirements in a clear and concise manner.

Furthermore, we will delve into the significance of collaboration and teamwork during the requirements gathering phase. Engineers must work closely with stakeholders, project managers, and other team members to ensure that all requirements are properly identified and documented. We will provide tips and strategies for facilitating effective collaboration and fostering a positive working environment.

Lastly, we will highlight the potential challenges and pitfalls that engineers may encounter during the requirements gathering and elicitation process. By recognizing these obstacles, engineers can proactively address them, minimizing the risk of misunderstandings or misalignments later in the development cycle.

By mastering the art of gathering and eliciting requirements, engineers in the field of Information Technology can significantly enhance the success rate of their software engineering projects. This subchapter aims to equip engineers with the necessary knowledge and skills to excel in this critical phase, ultimately resulting in the delivery of high-quality software solutions that meet the needs of end-users.

Requirements Analysis and Documentation

In the field of software engineering, the process of requirements analysis and documentation plays a crucial role in the successful development of software systems. This subchapter aims to provide engineers in the information technology niche with a comprehensive understanding of the importance of requirements analysis and the techniques involved in effectively documenting software requirements.

Requirements analysis is the initial phase of the software development life cycle that involves gathering, analyzing, and documenting the needs and constraints of stakeholders. It serves as the foundation for the entire software development process, ensuring that the final product meets user expectations and business requirements.

During the requirements analysis phase, engineers work closely with stakeholders to identify and prioritize functional and non-functional requirements. Functional requirements outline the specific features and functionalities that the software system must possess, while non-functional requirements focus on quality attributes such as performance, reliability, and security. By conducting interviews, workshops, and surveys, engineers can elicit requirements from stakeholders and gain a comprehensive understanding of their needs.

Once the requirements are identified, the next step is to document them accurately and comprehensively. Documentation serves as a reference for the development team and other stakeholders throughout the software development process. It helps in avoiding misunderstandings, aligning expectations, and tracking changes and updates.

Effective documentation should include clear and concise requirements statements, use cases, user stories, and diagrams. Engineers should utilize industry-standard notations and tools, such as Unified Modeling Language (UML), to create visual representations of the software system's architecture, behavior, and relationships.

Additionally, engineers must ensure that the documented requirements are testable and measurable. This allows for the creation of test cases and validation of the software system during the testing phase. By establishing traceability between requirements and test cases, engineers can ensure that all requirements are adequately validated.

In conclusion, requirements analysis and documentation are essential components of the software development process. By engaging in thorough requirements analysis and creating comprehensive documentation, engineers in the information technology niche can ensure the successful development and delivery of high-quality software systems. This subchapter provides a detailed exploration of the techniques and best practices involved in requirements analysis and documentation, empowering engineers to excel in their software engineering endeavors.

Validation and Verification of Requirements

In the realm of software engineering, the successful development of a high-quality software product heavily relies on the accurate and efficient validation and verification of requirements. This subchapter will delve into the crucial process of ensuring that the software requirements are thoroughly examined, validated, and verified before the development phase commences.

Validation is the process of evaluating the requirements to determine if they accurately capture the customer's needs and expectations. It involves analyzing the requirements against various criteria, such as completeness, consistency, clarity, and feasibility. Engineers play a pivotal role in this process by conducting comprehensive reviews, interviews, and discussions with stakeholders to validate the requirements. They must possess a deep understanding of the domain and technical expertise to identify any discrepancies, ambiguities, or conflicts within the requirements.

Verification, on the other hand, is the process of checking whether the requirements have been implemented correctly and whether the software product satisfies the specified requirements. Engineers employ various techniques, such as inspections, walkthroughs, and testing, to verify the requirements. They meticulously examine the software design, code, and test cases to ensure that they align with the requirements and conform to the specified standards and guidelines.

Effective validation and verification of requirements is essential for several reasons. Firstly, it helps in eliminating misunderstandings and misinterpretations, ensuring that the software product meets the customer's expectations. Secondly, it aids in identifying potential risks and issues early in the development process, enabling timely mitigation measures. Thirdly, it facilitates the creation of a solid foundation for the subsequent phases of the software development lifecycle, ensuring a smoother and more efficient development process.

Engineers in the field of Information Technology need to be well-versed in the techniques and tools employed for requirements validation and verification. They must possess strong analytical and problem-solving skills to identify and rectify any issues that may arise during this critical phase. Moreover, they should be adept at effective communication and collaboration, as they often need to work closely with stakeholders to gather feedback and ensure the requirements accurately reflect the desired software product.

By mastering the art of requirements validation and verification, engineers in the field of Information Technology can significantly enhance the quality and reliability of software products. This subchapter provides a comprehensive guide, equipping engineers with the necessary knowledge and skills to effectively validate and verify requirements, ultimately leading to the successful delivery of software solutions that meet customer expectations in the ever-evolving world of software engineering.

Chapter 4: Software Design Principles

Object-Oriented Design

In the realm of software engineering, Object-Oriented Design (OOD) is a crucial concept that allows engineers to create robust and scalable software systems. This subchapter will delve into the principles and techniques of OOD, providing engineers in the field of Information Technology with a comprehensive understanding of this essential design paradigm.

Object-Oriented Design is a methodology that revolves around the concept of objects, which are tangible representations of real-world entities. These objects encapsulate both data and the operations that can be performed on that data, enabling engineers to create modular and reusable code. By breaking down a software system into smaller, self-contained objects, developers can easily manage and maintain complex applications.

One of the fundamental principles of Object-Oriented Design is encapsulation. This principle emphasizes the bundling of data and methods within an object, allowing for better security, control, and reusability. Engineers can hide the internal details of an object, exposing only the necessary information and behavior to other objects. This promotes code modularity and reduces dependencies, making it easier to modify and update software systems as requirements evolve.

Another vital aspect of OOD is inheritance, which enables engineers to create new classes based on existing ones. Inheritance allows for the reuse of code, reducing redundancy and enhancing code maintainability. By inheriting the characteristics of a base class, engineers can build specialized classes, fostering code extensibility and flexibility.

Polymorphism is yet another important concept in Object-Oriented Design. It refers to the ability of objects to take on multiple forms or exhibit different behaviors based on the context. Polymorphism enables engineers to write generic code that can work with different types of objects, enhancing code reusability and adaptability.

To effectively apply OOD, engineers must also understand the importance of design patterns. These are reusable solutions to commonly occurring design problems. By leveraging design patterns, engineers can solve complex design challenges efficiently and effectively, ensuring the creation of robust and maintainable software systems.

In conclusion, Object-Oriented Design is a critical aspect of software engineering for engineers working in the Information Technology niche. By embracing the principles of encapsulation, inheritance, and polymorphism, engineers can create modular, reusable, and scalable software systems. Understanding and applying design patterns further enhances the quality and maintainability of these systems. By mastering Object-Oriented Design, engineers can elevate their software engineering skills and deliver high-quality solutions in the dynamic field of Information Technology.

Design Patterns

In the ever-evolving field of Information Technology, engineers often face complex problems that require creative and efficient solutions. This is where design patterns come into play. Design patterns are reusable solutions to commonly occurring problems in software design and development. They provide engineers with proven strategies to tackle challenges and improve the overall quality of their code.

This subchapter aims to introduce engineers to the concept of design patterns and their significance in mastering software engineering. It will delve into the different types of design patterns and their practical applications, empowering engineers to make informed decisions and write robust, maintainable code.

The subchapter begins by exploring the fundamentals of design patterns, explaining how they encapsulate best practices and provide a framework for solving recurring problems. It highlights the importance of design patterns in promoting code reusability, readability, and modularity. By leveraging design patterns, engineers can optimize their development process, reduce bugs, and enhance collaboration within teams.

Next, the subchapter delves into the three main categories of design patterns: creational, structural, and behavioral patterns. Creational patterns focus on object creation mechanisms, ensuring that objects are created in a flexible and efficient manner. Structural patterns deal with class and object composition, allowing engineers to build complex structures while keeping their code flexible and maintainable.

Behavioral patterns, on the other hand, focus on communication between objects, enabling engineers to define how objects interact and fulfill their responsibilities.

Throughout the subchapter, real-world examples and case studies are provided to illustrate the practical applications of design patterns. Engineers will learn to identify common design problems and apply appropriate design patterns to solve them effectively. Additionally, the subchapter discusses potential pitfalls and anti-patterns that engineers should be aware of, helping them avoid common mistakes and improve their software engineering skills.

By the end of this subchapter, engineers will have a comprehensive understanding of design patterns and their role in mastering software engineering. They will be equipped with the knowledge and tools to analyze complex problems, select appropriate design patterns, and implement elegant solutions. Whether working on large-scale software projects or small-scale applications, engineers will be able to leverage design patterns to create robust, scalable, and maintainable code.

Architectural Design

In the dynamic field of information technology, architectural design plays a pivotal role in the development of robust and scalable software systems. It is an essential discipline that enables engineers to create software architectures that meet the complex requirements of today's industry.

This subchapter on architectural design aims to provide engineers in the information technology niche with a comprehensive understanding of the principles, methodologies, and best practices involved in designing effective software architectures.

The subchapter begins by introducing the fundamental concepts of architectural design, highlighting its significance in the software engineering process. It emphasizes the need for engineers to approach software design with a holistic mindset, considering factors such as system performance, scalability, maintainability, and security.

The subchapter then delves into various architectural design patterns and styles commonly used in the industry. It explores the benefits and drawbacks of each pattern, providing engineers with the knowledge to select the most appropriate architecture for a given project. Topics covered include layered architectures, client-server architectures, microservices, and event-driven architectures.

To supplement theoretical knowledge, practical examples and case studies are included throughout the subchapter. These real-world scenarios help engineers grasp the application of architectural design principles in different contexts, enabling them to make informed design decisions.

Furthermore, the subchapter delves into the process of architectural design, outlining key steps and techniques for creating effective software architectures. It covers requirements analysis, system decomposition, interface design, and architectural documentation. It emphasizes the importance of collaboration and communication among stakeholders throughout the design process.

Lastly, the subchapter explores emerging trends and technologies in architectural design, such as cloud computing, containerization, and service-oriented architectures. It highlights their impact on software architecture and provides insights into leveraging these technologies effectively.

By the end of this subchapter, engineers in the information technology niche will have a solid foundation in architectural design. They will be equipped with the knowledge and skills necessary to create robust, scalable, and maintainable software architectures that meet the demands of today's rapidly evolving industry.

Component-Based Design

In today's fast-paced world of Information Technology (IT), engineers face the challenge of developing software systems that are not only efficient and reliable but also easily maintainable and scalable. Component-Based Design (CBD) is a methodology that provides a solution to these challenges by breaking down complex systems into smaller, reusable components.

CBD is a design approach that promotes the modularization of software systems, enabling engineers to build applications by combining pre-existing software components. These components encapsulate specific functionalities and can be developed independently, allowing for easier testing, maintenance, and reusability. By utilizing CBD, engineers can save time and effort in the development process, as they can focus on building components that are already well-tested and proven to be reliable.

One of the key advantages of CBD is the flexibility it offers. Engineers can select and assemble components based on the specific requirements of their project, resulting in highly customizable and scalable software systems. This modular approach also enhances system maintainability, as modifications or updates can be made to individual components without affecting the entire system. Additionally, CBD facilitates code reuse, reducing redundancy and promoting efficiency in software development.

To implement CBD successfully, engineers must follow certain principles. Firstly, components should have well-defined interfaces that clearly specify their inputs, outputs, and functionalities. This helps in ensuring compatibility and interoperability between different components. Secondly, engineers should consider the granularity of the components, ensuring that they are neither too fine-grained nor too coarse-grained. Finding the right balance allows for optimal reusability and flexibility. Lastly, engineers should establish a robust component repository, where well-documented and thoroughly tested components can be stored and easily accessed by the development team.

While CBD offers numerous benefits, it is essential for engineers to be aware of its limitations. For instance, not all software systems are suitable for CBD. Complex systems with tightly coupled components may not lend themselves well to modularization. Additionally, engineers must carefully evaluate the quality and reliability of the components they choose to integrate into their systems, as the overall system's performance may be affected by the quality of these components.

In conclusion, Component-Based Design is a powerful methodology that can greatly enhance the development process for engineers in the field of Information Technology. By leveraging pre-existing components, engineers can build efficient, scalable, and maintainable software systems. However, a thoughtful approach is necessary to ensure the successful implementation of CBD, taking into consideration factors such as component granularity, interface design, and component quality. With proper understanding and application, engineers can master the art of Component-Based Design and elevate their software engineering skills to the next level.

Chapter 5: Software Development Tools and Technologies

Integrated Development Environments (IDEs)

In the rapidly evolving field of Information Technology, engineers play a crucial role in developing software solutions that power our modern world. To effectively manage the complexities of software development, engineers rely on Integrated Development Environments (IDEs) - powerful tools that streamline the coding process and enhance productivity.

An IDE is a software application that provides a comprehensive set of features and tools specifically designed to assist engineers in writing, debugging, and maintaining code. It serves as a centralized platform where engineers can write, compile, run, and test their code in a single environment. IDEs offer a seamless integration of various development tools, making them indispensable for software engineers.

One of the primary advantages of using an IDE is its ability to provide a highly efficient coding experience. With features like code completion, syntax highlighting, and intelligent error detection, engineers can write code faster and with fewer mistakes. IDEs also offer powerful debugging capabilities, allowing engineers to step through their code, set breakpoints, and analyze variables, making the process of identifying and fixing issues much easier.

Furthermore, IDEs simplify the process of managing large projects. They provide features such as project management, version control integration, and build automation, which facilitate collaboration among team members and ensure the smooth development of complex software systems. This centralized approach saves engineers valuable time by reducing the need to switch between multiple tools and platforms.

IDEs cater to a wide range of programming languages and frameworks, making them versatile tools for engineers across various domains of Information Technology. Whether you're developing web applications using languages like HTML, CSS, and JavaScript, or building complex systems with languages like Java, Python, or C++, IDEs offer tailored functionalities to suit your needs.

As an engineer, it is essential to master the usage of IDEs to maximize your productivity and efficiency. Familiarizing yourself with the features and capabilities of popular IDEs such as Eclipse, Visual Studio, or IntelliJ IDEA will provide you with a competitive edge in the dynamic field of software engineering.

In conclusion, Integrated Development Environments (IDEs) are indispensable tools for engineers working in the field of Information Technology. They offer a centralized platform that enhances coding efficiency, simplifies project management, and facilitates collaboration. By leveraging the power of IDEs, engineers can streamline their software development process and stay ahead in an ever-evolving industry.

Version Control Systems

In the ever-evolving field of Information Technology, software engineers are constantly faced with the challenge of managing the various versions of their code. This is where Version Control Systems (VCS) come into play. VCS is a fundamental tool that allows engineers to track changes in their code, collaborate with team members, and ensure the integrity of their projects. In this subchapter, we will delve into the intricacies of Version Control Systems and explore why they are essential for engineers in the field of Information Technology.

First and foremost, a Version Control System enables engineers to keep track of changes made to their code over time. By using a VCS, engineers can easily revert back to previous versions of their code, should any issues arise. This not only provides a safety net for experimentation but also ensures that teams can work on different features simultaneously without fear of losing any progress. Additionally, VCS allows engineers to annotate and comment on code changes, providing valuable insights into the rationale behind each modification.

Collaboration is another crucial aspect of software engineering, especially in the Information Technology sector. Version Control Systems facilitate seamless collaboration among team members by providing a centralized repository where everyone can contribute their code. Through features like branching and merging, engineers can work on different aspects of a project simultaneously, ensuring efficient teamwork and minimizing conflicts.

Ensuring the integrity and stability of the software is of paramount importance. With a Version Control System, engineers can enforce strict quality control measures. By making use of features like code reviews and continuous integration, software engineers can catch potential issues early on and ensure that only stable and error-free code makes its way into the final product. Moreover, VCS provides a comprehensive audit trail, allowing engineers to trace the evolution of their code and identify any potential vulnerabilities.

In conclusion, Version Control Systems play a crucial role in the field of Information Technology by providing engineers with a robust set of tools to manage and track changes in their code. From facilitating collaboration and ensuring the integrity of the software to enabling efficient teamwork and maintaining a comprehensive audit trail, VCS is an indispensable tool for any software engineer. By mastering Version Control Systems, engineers can streamline their development process, enhance code quality, and ultimately deliver exceptional software solutions.

Test Automation Tools

In today's fast-paced and dynamic world of Information Technology, engineers are constantly challenged to deliver high-quality software solutions within tight deadlines. The need for efficient and effective testing methodologies has never been more critical. This is where test automation tools come into play.

Test automation tools are software applications that help engineers automate the testing process, reducing the overall effort and time required for testing while improving accuracy and reliability. These tools enable engineers to create, execute, and analyze tests automatically, allowing them to focus on more complex and critical aspects of software development.

One of the major advantages of test automation tools is their ability to perform repetitive tasks quickly and accurately. Engineers can write test scripts using various programming languages or use a graphical user interface (GUI) to create tests. These tools provide a wide range of features, including record and playback, script generation, data-driven testing, and the creation of test suites. By automating repetitive tasks, engineers can significantly reduce human errors and increase the overall efficiency of the testing process.

Another key advantage of test automation tools is their ability to execute tests across multiple platforms and environments. With the ever-increasing complexity of software systems, engineers must ensure that their applications work seamlessly on different operating systems, browsers, and devices. Test automation tools provide the flexibility to run tests on various platforms simultaneously, allowing engineers to identify and fix compatibility issues early in the development cycle.

Furthermore, test automation tools provide detailed reports and metrics, enabling engineers to analyze test results comprehensively. These tools generate logs, screenshots, and performance metrics, helping engineers identify bottlenecks, memory leaks, and other potential issues. By analyzing these reports, engineers can make informed decisions and prioritize their efforts, resulting in improved software quality.

While test automation tools offer numerous benefits, it is important to note that they are not a silver bullet solution. Engineers must carefully select the appropriate tool based on their specific requirements, budget, and technical expertise. Additionally, regular maintenance and updates are necessary to ensure that the tools remain compatible with evolving software technologies.

In conclusion, test automation tools have become an indispensable part of the software engineering process. As engineers strive to deliver high-quality software solutions in the fast-paced world of Information Technology, these tools provide the means to automate testing tasks, improve efficiency, and enhance overall software quality. By embracing test automation tools, engineers can focus their efforts on innovation and problem-solving, ultimately delivering superior software products to their customers.

Collaboration and Project Management Tools

In today's fast-paced and interconnected world, effective collaboration and project management are essential for the success of any software engineering endeavor. With the advent of sophisticated technology, engineers in the field of Information Technology (IT) have access to a wide range of tools that can greatly enhance their collaboration efforts and streamline project management processes. This subchapter explores some of the most popular collaboration and project management tools available to engineers in the IT industry.

One of the most widely used tools in this domain is project management software. These software applications provide engineers with a centralized platform to plan, track, and manage project workflows, tasks, and deadlines. They often come equipped with features such as Gantt charts, task assignment and tracking, resource management, and communication tools. Popular project management software includes Microsoft Project, Jira, and Asana. Understanding how to effectively utilize these tools can greatly improve an engineer's ability to stay organized and meet project milestones.

In addition to project management software, engineers can also benefit from collaboration tools that facilitate effective communication and teamwork. These tools enable engineers to collaborate on code, share documents, and exchange ideas in real-time. Version control systems like Git allow engineers to work together on code repositories, ensuring seamless integration and minimizing conflicts. Tools like Slack and Microsoft Teams provide instant messaging, video conferencing, and file-sharing capabilities that promote effective communication and foster collaboration among team members, regardless of their physical locations.

Moreover, engineers can leverage cloud-based platforms to enhance collaboration and project management. Platforms like Google Drive and Dropbox enable engineers to store and share project files securely, ensuring that team members have access to the most up-to-date documents. Cloud-based project management tools, such as Trello and Basecamp, offer added flexibility by allowing engineers to access project-related information from anywhere, anytime.

In conclusion, collaboration and project management tools are indispensable for engineers in the field of Information Technology. The availability of advanced software applications, collaboration tools, and cloud-based platforms has revolutionized the way engineers work together, improving productivity, efficiency, and overall project success. By mastering these tools and incorporating them into their workflows, engineers can stay ahead in the dynamic and competitive world of software engineering.

Chapter 6: Software Testing and Quality Assurance

Testing Techniques and Strategies

In the fast-paced world of information technology, software engineering has become an integral part of our everyday lives. As engineers in this field, it is crucial for us to ensure that the software we develop is robust, reliable, and meets the needs and expectations of our users. This is where testing techniques and strategies come into play.

Testing is a critical phase in the software development life cycle, allowing us to identify and rectify any defects or bugs in the software before it is deployed. It helps ensure that the software performs as expected, meets the specified requirements, and delivers a seamless user experience. In this subchapter, we will explore various testing techniques and strategies that can be employed to achieve these goals.

Firstly, we will delve into unit testing, which involves testing individual components or modules of the software in isolation. By verifying the correctness and functionality of each unit, we can identify and fix any defects early on in the development process. This helps in reducing the overall cost and effort required for bug fixing.

Next, we will discuss integration testing, where multiple units are tested together to ensure that they work harmoniously and produce the desired output. This type of testing helps in identifying any issues that may arise due to the interaction between different modules.

Furthermore, we will explore system testing, which involves testing the software as a whole, simulating real-world scenarios and user interactions. This type of testing helps in validating the software against the specified requirements and ensures that it performs seamlessly in different environments.

In addition to these techniques, we will also cover performance testing, security testing, and usability testing. Performance testing allows us to evaluate the software's responsiveness, scalability, and resource utilization under varying workloads. Security testing helps in identifying vulnerabilities and ensuring that the software is protected against potential threats. Usability testing focuses on assessing the software's user-friendliness and ease of navigation.

Throughout this subchapter, we will delve into practical strategies and best practices for effective testing. We will explore test planning, test case design, test automation, and defect tracking. By adopting these strategies, engineers can enhance the efficiency and reliability of their testing processes.

In conclusion, mastering testing techniques and strategies is essential for engineers in the information technology niche. It enables us to deliver high-quality software that meets user expectations and withstands real-world challenges. Through this subchapter, we aim to equip engineers with the necessary knowledge and skills to excel in software testing and ensure the success of their projects.

Test Planning and Execution

In the fast-paced world of information technology, where software development is a critical component, the importance of effective test planning and execution cannot be overstated. As engineers in this ever-evolving field, it is crucial to understand the significance of thorough testing to deliver high-quality software solutions. This subchapter aims to provide you, as an engineer in the niche of information technology, with comprehensive insights and guidance on test planning and execution to master the art of software engineering.

Test planning involves creating a roadmap that outlines the testing activities required to validate the software. It starts with understanding the project requirements and identifying the testing objectives. By defining clear and achievable goals, you can ensure that your testing efforts align with the project's overall objectives. This subchapter will delve into the various components of test planning, including test strategy, test scope, test estimation, and resource allocation.

Once the test planning phase is complete, the focus shifts to test execution. This phase involves the actual implementation of the planned tests, monitoring and analyzing test results, and reporting defects found during testing. We will explore different testing techniques such as black-box testing, white-box testing, and gray-box testing, enabling you to choose the most appropriate approach for your specific project.

To master test planning and execution, it is essential to understand the importance of test automation. We will discuss the benefits of test automation, the selection of suitable automation tools, and best practices for creating robust and maintainable automated test suites. Additionally, this subchapter will cover the integration of automated tests into the overall software development lifecycle, ensuring continuous testing and feedback loops.

Furthermore, we will provide insights into effective test case design, including techniques for identifying test scenarios and creating test cases that cover the maximum possible functional and non-functional aspects of the software.

Throughout this subchapter, real-world examples and case studies will be used to illustrate the concepts and techniques discussed. By leveraging the knowledge and best practices shared in this subchapter, you will be well-equipped to plan and execute tests effectively, leading to the delivery of high-quality software solutions in the fast-paced world of information technology.

Remember, as engineers in the field of information technology, your expertise goes beyond writing code. Mastering test planning and execution will undoubtedly set you apart as a highly skilled software engineer.

Defect Tracking and Management

In the fast-paced world of information technology, software defects are an inevitable part of the development process. These defects, also known as bugs, can have a significant impact on the functionality and performance of software applications. Therefore, it is imperative for engineers to have a solid understanding of defect tracking and management techniques to ensure the successful delivery of high-quality software products.

Defect tracking refers to the process of identifying, documenting, and monitoring software defects throughout the development lifecycle. It involves capturing detailed information about each defect, including its symptoms, severity, and potential impact on the system. Engineers use various tools and techniques to track defects, allowing them to prioritize and address them in a systematic manner.

One crucial aspect of defect tracking is the use of a defect tracking system or software. These systems provide a centralized repository for recording and managing defects, making it easier for engineers to track their progress and assign tasks to team members. With a defect tracking system in place, engineers can ensure that defects are not overlooked or forgotten, reducing the risk of critical issues slipping through the cracks.

Effective defect management is equally important in ensuring the timely resolution of defects. Engineers must establish a well-defined process for managing defects, including steps for reporting, triaging, and resolving them. This process should involve regular communication and collaboration with stakeholders, including developers, testers, and project managers, to ensure a coordinated effort in defect resolution.

In addition to tracking and managing defects, engineers should also focus on preventing them from occurring in the first place. This can be achieved through rigorous testing and quality assurance practices, including code reviews, unit testing, and system integration testing. By catching and addressing defects early in the development cycle, engineers can minimize the impact on the final software product.

In conclusion, defect tracking and management are critical components of the software engineering process. Engineers in the field of information technology must be well-versed in these techniques to ensure the delivery of high-quality software products. By effectively tracking and managing defects, engineers can minimize the impact of software defects, enhance customer satisfaction, and ultimately contribute to the success of their organizations.

Continuous Integration and Continuous Delivery (CI/CD)

In today's fast-paced world of Information Technology, the ability to deliver high-quality software products quickly and reliably is crucial for any organization. This is where Continuous Integration and Continuous Delivery (CI/CD) practices come into play. CI/CD is a set of software development practices that help engineers automate the process of building, testing, and deploying their applications. By adopting CI/CD, engineers can ensure that their code is always in a releasable state and ready to be deployed to production at any given moment.

Continuous Integration is the practice of frequently merging code changes from multiple developers into a shared repository. This allows engineers to detect and fix integration issues early on, reducing the risk of conflicts and ensuring that the application remains stable. By automating the process of code integration, engineers can eliminate the time-consuming and error-prone manual merging process.

Continuous Delivery, on the other hand, focuses on automating the release process of software. It enables engineers to deploy their applications to production environments quickly and easily. With Continuous Delivery, engineers can ensure that the code is always in a deployable state by automating the build, testing, and deployment processes. This not only speeds up the time to market but also reduces the chances of introducing bugs and other issues into the production environment.

CI/CD practices rely heavily on automation and the use of tools and technologies to streamline the development and deployment processes. Continuous Integration tools like Jenkins, Travis CI, and CircleCI automate the process of building and testing code changes. They enable engineers to run unit tests, integration tests, and other forms of automated testing to ensure the quality of the code. Continuous Delivery tools like Kubernetes and Docker help engineers automate the deployment process by providing consistent and reliable environments for running applications.

By adopting CI/CD practices, engineers can significantly improve the speed, reliability, and quality of their software development processes. It allows them to focus on writing code and developing new features rather than spending time on manual and repetitive tasks. CI/CD also promotes collaboration and communication among team members, as it encourages frequent code integration and sharing of feedback. With CI/CD, engineers can deliver software products faster, with fewer defects, and with more confidence.

In conclusion, Continuous Integration and Continuous Delivery (CI/CD) practices have become essential for engineers in the field of Information Technology. By automating the process of code integration and deployment, CI/CD enables engineers to deliver high-quality software products quickly and reliably. With the help of various tools and technologies, engineers can streamline their development processes, reduce the risk of conflicts and bugs, and ultimately improve the efficiency and productivity of their teams.

Chapter 7: Software Maintenance and Evolution

Software Maintenance Processes

In the fast-paced world of technology, software engineering plays a critical role in the development and maintenance of various software applications. As engineers in the field of information technology, it is essential to understand the importance of software maintenance processes. This subchapter aims to provide a comprehensive guide to mastering software maintenance processes and their significance in the field.

Software maintenance refers to the modification, enhancement, and bug fixing of existing software applications. It is an integral part of the software development life cycle (SDLC) and ensures that software continues to function optimally and meet the evolving needs of users. In this subchapter, we will delve into the various processes involved in software maintenance and explore their relevance in the world of engineering.

The subchapter will begin by discussing the types of software maintenance processes, namely corrective, adaptive, perfective, and preventive maintenance. Each type addresses specific aspects of software maintenance, such as fixing defects, adapting to changes in the environment, improving functionality, and preventing future issues. Understanding these processes is crucial for engineers to effectively manage software maintenance tasks.

Furthermore, the subchapter will explore the key activities involved in software maintenance, including bug tracking, impact analysis, code refactoring, and regression testing. These activities ensure that software changes are implemented smoothly and do not introduce new issues into the system.

Additionally, the subchapter will provide insights into the challenges and best practices of software maintenance. Engineers will learn about the importance of documentation, version control, and collaboration in maintaining software efficiently. They will also gain an understanding of the need for proper planning, resource allocation, and risk management to overcome common obstacles in the maintenance process.

To enhance the learning experience, real-world examples and case studies will be included throughout the subchapter. These examples will showcase how software maintenance processes have been successfully implemented in various information technology niches, highlighting the positive impact on software quality, user satisfaction, and overall productivity.

By the end of this subchapter, engineers will have a comprehensive understanding of the software maintenance processes and their significance in the field of information technology. Armed with this knowledge, they will be well-equipped to handle the challenges that arise during software maintenance, ensuring the longevity and success of software applications.

Enhancement and Modification of Existing Software

Subchapter: Enhancement and Modification of Existing Software

Introduction:
In the ever-evolving field of information technology, software engineering plays a crucial role in developing and maintaining software systems. As engineers, it is essential to understand the process of enhancing and modifying existing software to meet changing user requirements and technological advancements. This subchapter aims to provide a comprehensive guide on this topic, enabling engineers to master the art of enhancing and modifying software effectively.

Understanding the Need for Enhancement and Modification: Software systems are not static; they constantly require updates and modifications to adapt to changing business needs, user expectations, and emerging technologies. Engineers must recognize that enhancement and modification are integral parts of the software lifecycle, ensuring the longevity and relevance of the software in a rapidly evolving IT landscape.

Key Factors to Consider:
Before embarking on any software enhancement or modification project, engineers must carefully evaluate several critical factors. These include the identification of user requirements, understanding the existing software architecture, assessing the impact on other components or systems, ensuring compatibility with hardware and software platforms, and estimating the potential risks and challenges involved.

Planning and Execution:
An effective enhancement or modification process starts with meticulous planning. Engineers should define clear objectives, establish a realistic timeline, allocate necessary resources, and prioritize tasks based on the desired outcome. Effective communication with stakeholders, including end-users, management, and other relevant parties, is vital for successful planning and execution.

Implementing Best Practices:
To ensure efficient enhancement and modification, engineers should adopt industry best practices. These include version control, code documentation, automated testing, and deployment strategies. A systematic approach that adheres to software engineering principles, such as modular design, separation of concerns, and maintainability, helps minimize errors, improve efficiency, and streamline the overall process.

Managing Risks and Challenges:
Enhancing or modifying existing software can be a complex task, often involving risks and challenges. Engineers must proactively identify potential risks and devise mitigation strategies. This may involve conducting thorough impact analysis, thorough testing, and ensuring a robust rollback plan in case of failures. Continuous monitoring and feedback loops throughout the enhancement process are essential to address issues promptly and minimize potential disruptions.

Conclusion:
Enhancement and modification of existing software are indispensable aspects of software engineering in the information technology domain.

By following the best practices, careful planning, and effective execution, engineers can ensure that software systems remain adaptable, scalable, and relevant. This subchapter has equipped engineers with the necessary knowledge and guidance to master the art of enhancing and modifying software, enabling them to thrive in the fast-paced world of IT.

Legacy System Modernization

In the ever-evolving world of information technology, the need to modernize legacy systems has become a pressing concern for engineers. Legacy systems, often characterized by outdated technologies, inefficient processes, and limited scalability, can hinder an organization's ability to adapt to changing business requirements and technological advancements. This subchapter will delve into the intricacies of legacy system modernization, providing engineers with a comprehensive guide to navigate this challenging process.

Legacy system modernization is the process of updating or replacing outdated software systems to enhance their functionality, improve performance, and align them with current business needs and technological trends. It involves a series of steps, including legacy system assessment, planning, design, migration, and testing. Each step is crucial in ensuring a successful modernization effort that minimizes disruptions and maximizes benefits.

This subchapter will begin by discussing the importance of legacy system modernization in the context of information technology. It will highlight the risks associated with maintaining legacy systems, such as increased maintenance costs, security vulnerabilities, and limited integration capabilities. By understanding these risks, engineers will be motivated to embark on the modernization journey.

Next, the subchapter will explore the key challenges and considerations when undertaking legacy system modernization. It will address issues such as system complexity, data migration, legacy code dependencies, and user adoption. By providing insights into these challenges, engineers will be better equipped to plan and execute successful modernization projects.

Furthermore, the subchapter will cover various modernization approaches and strategies, including system reengineering, componentization, service-oriented architecture (SOA), and cloud migration. It will discuss the pros and cons of each approach, providing engineers with a comprehensive overview of available options.

To ensure a smooth modernization process, the subchapter will also delve into best practices and methodologies. It will explore topics such as incremental modernization, agile methodologies, and the importance of collaboration between engineers, business stakeholders, and end-users.

Lastly, the subchapter will conclude with a discussion on the potential benefits and return on investment (ROI) of legacy system modernization. It will highlight success stories and real-world examples, showcasing the transformative power of modernization efforts.

By mastering the art of legacy system modernization, engineers in the field of information technology can unlock the true potential of organizations, enabling them to stay competitive in an ever-changing digital landscape.

Software Retirement and Decommissioning

In the fast-paced world of Information Technology, software applications play a crucial role in enabling businesses to streamline their operations, improve efficiency, and deliver innovative solutions. However, just as software is developed and implemented, there comes a time when it reaches the end of its useful life and needs to be retired and decommissioned. This subchapter explores the process of software retirement and decommissioning, providing engineers in the field of Information Technology with a comprehensive guide.

Software retirement refers to the planned and systematic process of discontinuing a software application, removing it from production, and ensuring its safe and secure removal from the organization's infrastructure. The decision to retire software can be driven by various factors, such as technological advancements rendering the software obsolete, changing business needs, or the introduction of more efficient and cost-effective alternatives.

The first step in software retirement is conducting a thorough assessment of the application's functionality, usage, and dependencies. This assessment helps engineers gain a clear understanding of the software's impact on the organization and identify any potential risks or challenges that may arise during the retirement process. It is crucial to involve key stakeholders, including end-users, IT staff, and management, to gather insights and ensure a smooth transition.

Once the assessment is complete, engineers can develop a detailed retirement plan. This plan outlines the necessary steps, timelines, and resources required to retire the software effectively. It includes activities such as data migration, system cleanup, user communication and training, and the establishment of proper documentation and archiving processes.

During the retirement process, engineers must ensure that all data and sensitive information stored within the software are appropriately transferred or securely deleted. This includes taking backups, migrating data to new systems, or securely disposing of data in accordance with the organization's data management policies and legal requirements.

Communication plays a vital role in software retirement. Engineers should keep all stakeholders informed about the retirement process, including the reasons behind the decision, timelines, and any impact on their workflows. Clear and timely communication helps manage expectations and minimizes disruptions during the transition.

After the software's retirement, engineers should conduct a post-implementation review to assess the effectiveness and efficiency of the retirement process. This review provides valuable insights for future retirements and helps identify areas for improvement.

In conclusion, software retirement and decommissioning are essential aspects of managing the lifecycle of software applications in the field of Information Technology. By following a systematic and well-planned approach, engineers can ensure a smooth and secure retirement, minimizing disruptions and maximizing the organization's technology investments.

Chapter 8: Software Project Management

Project Planning and Estimation

In the dynamic and fast-paced field of Information Technology (IT), project planning and estimation play a crucial role in ensuring the success of software engineering endeavors. Properly planning and estimating projects can help engineers effectively allocate resources, manage timelines, and deliver high-quality solutions that meet clients' requirements.

This subchapter of "Mastering Software Engineering: A Comprehensive Guide for Engineers" dives deep into the intricacies of project planning and estimation, equipping IT professionals with the necessary knowledge and skills to navigate the complexities of software development projects.

The subchapter begins by introducing the fundamental concepts of project planning, emphasizing the importance of defining clear objectives, scope, and deliverables. Engineers will learn how to break down complex projects into manageable tasks, create realistic project schedules, and establish effective communication channels to ensure collaboration among team members.

The subchapter also delves into the estimation process, a critical aspect of project planning. Engineers will learn various estimation techniques, such as the widely used bottom-up and top-down approaches, as well as how to leverage historical data and industry benchmarks to improve accuracy. They will also explore the concept of effort estimation, considering factors such as project complexity, team skills, and resource availability.

Additionally, the subchapter delves into risk management, an integral part of project planning. Engineers will discover how to identify potential risks, assess their potential impact, and develop mitigation strategies to minimize their effects. They will also explore techniques for prioritizing risks and creating contingency plans to ensure project resilience.

Throughout the subchapter, real-life case studies and examples provide practical insights into the challenges and strategies involved in project planning and estimation. The content is presented in a concise and accessible manner, ensuring that engineers can easily apply the concepts and techniques to their own projects.

By mastering the art of project planning and estimation, IT engineers can enhance their ability to deliver successful software engineering projects. Whether working on large-scale enterprise solutions or small-scale applications, this subchapter equips engineers with the tools and knowledge needed to consistently deliver high-quality software solutions on time and within budget.

Resource Allocation and Management

Effective resource allocation and management are vital components of successful software engineering projects in the field of information technology. In this subchapter, we will delve into the importance of resource allocation and explore strategies for managing resources efficiently.

Resource allocation refers to the process of assigning available resources, such as human capital, time, and budget, to specific tasks and activities within a project. It involves identifying the needs of the project and making informed decisions about how to allocate resources effectively to meet those needs.

For engineers working in the field of information technology, resource allocation is particularly critical due to the dynamic nature of software development projects. With ever-changing requirements, tight deadlines, and limited resources, engineers must be adept at managing resources to ensure project success.

One of the key strategies for resource allocation is conducting a thorough project analysis. This involves identifying the project's scope, objectives, and requirements while considering the available resources. By understanding the project's needs and limitations from the outset, engineers can make more informed decisions regarding resource allocation.

Another important aspect of resource management is prioritization. Engineers must prioritize tasks and activities based on their importance and urgency. This ensures that critical tasks are given the necessary resources and attention, while less critical ones are appropriately managed. Prioritization helps avoid resource wastage and enables engineers to focus on activities that contribute most to the project's success.

Furthermore, effective communication and collaboration play a vital role in resource management. Engineers need to communicate with team members and stakeholders to ensure that resources are allocated efficiently and that everyone is aware of the project's progress. Collaborative decision-making allows for better resource allocation by leveraging the expertise and insights of all team members.

In addition, engineers can utilize various tools and techniques for resource allocation and management. Project management software, such as Gantt charts and resource tracking tools, can provide real-time visibility into resource allocation and utilization. These tools enable engineers to monitor resource usage, identify bottlenecks, and make adjustments as needed.

In conclusion, resource allocation and management are crucial skills for engineers working in the field of information technology. By thoroughly analyzing projects, prioritizing tasks, fostering effective communication, and utilizing appropriate tools, engineers can optimize resource allocation and enhance the success of software engineering projects.

Risk Management

In the fast-paced world of information technology, risk management plays a crucial role in ensuring the successful execution of software engineering projects. As engineers, it is essential for us to understand the importance of identifying, assessing, and mitigating risks throughout the development lifecycle. This subchapter will delve into the realm of risk management, equipping you with the knowledge and tools necessary to navigate the complexities of software engineering in the field of information technology.

Risk management is a systematic and proactive approach that involves identifying potential risks, analyzing their potential impact, and implementing strategies to minimize or eliminate them. It encompasses a wide range of activities, from risk identification and assessment to risk monitoring and control. By effectively managing risks, engineers can enhance project outcomes, reduce the likelihood of failures, and improve overall project success rates.

This subchapter will introduce you to various techniques and methodologies used in risk management, such as risk identification matrices, risk assessment frameworks, and risk mitigation strategies. You will learn how to identify and categorize risks based on their probability and impact, enabling you to prioritize and allocate resources accordingly. Moreover, you will gain insights into different risk response strategies, including risk avoidance, risk transfer, risk mitigation, and risk acceptance.

Furthermore, this subchapter will explore the integration of risk management into the software engineering process. You will understand how risk management activities are intertwined with other project management processes, such as requirements gathering, design, development, testing, and deployment. We will discuss how to incorporate risk management practices into each phase of the software development lifecycle, ensuring that risks are addressed early on and not left to chance.

In conclusion, risk management is an integral part of software engineering in the field of information technology. By embracing a proactive approach to identifying, assessing, and mitigating risks, engineers can ensure the successful delivery of software projects. This subchapter will equip you with the necessary knowledge and tools to navigate the complexities of risk management in software engineering, empowering you to make informed decisions and effectively manage risks throughout the development lifecycle.

Agile Project Management

In today's fast-paced world of Information Technology, traditional project management approaches are often seen as rigid and cumbersome. As engineers, we need to be equipped with the knowledge and skills to navigate the ever-changing landscape of software development. This is where Agile Project Management comes into play.

Agile Project Management is a flexible and iterative approach to managing software development projects. It emphasizes collaboration, adaptability, and continuous improvement. Unlike traditional project management methods that follow a strict waterfall model, Agile allows for evolving requirements and encourages frequent feedback from stakeholders. This iterative process ensures that the project stays on track and delivers value to the end-users.

One of the key principles of Agile Project Management is the use of short development cycles called sprints. These sprints typically last for two to four weeks, during which the development team focuses on a set of prioritized user stories or features. At the end of each sprint, the team reviews the progress, incorporates feedback, and adjusts the project plan accordingly. This incremental approach allows for early and frequent delivery of working software, enabling faster time-to-market and increased customer satisfaction.

Another important aspect of Agile Project Management is the concept of self-organizing teams. Unlike traditional hierarchical structures, Agile teams are empowered to make decisions and take ownership of their work. This promotes collaboration and fosters a sense of shared responsibility among team members. By empowering engineers to have a say in project planning and execution, Agile Project Management enhances creativity, innovation, and overall team morale.

To successfully implement Agile Project Management, engineers need to adopt specific practices and tools. These include user story mapping, sprint planning, daily stand-up meetings, and retrospectives. Additionally, various Agile frameworks such as Scrum, Kanban, and Lean can be used to guide the project management process and ensure its effectiveness.

In conclusion, Agile Project Management is a vital skill for engineers in the field of Information Technology. By embracing the principles of collaboration, adaptability, and continuous improvement, Agile enables us to deliver high-quality software products that meet the changing needs of our customers. So, let's dive into the world of Agile Project Management and master this powerful approach to software engineering.

Chapter 9: Software Engineering Ethics and Professionalism

Ethical Dilemmas in Software Engineering

In the rapidly evolving field of information technology, software engineering has become a vital discipline. As engineers in this domain, it is crucial to understand and navigate the ethical dilemmas that may arise in our profession. This subchapter explores some of the ethical challenges faced by software engineers and provides guidance on how to approach them.

One of the primary ethical considerations in software engineering is privacy and data protection. Engineers often handle sensitive user information, and it is our responsibility to ensure its confidentiality and security. However, we may encounter dilemmas when organizations demand access to user data for various purposes. Balancing the rights and interests of users with the needs of the organization can be challenging, and engineers must be prepared to advocate for user privacy rights while meeting business requirements.

Another ethical dilemma arises in the context of intellectual property. Software engineers work with copyrighted code and proprietary technologies. It is essential to understand and respect intellectual property laws to avoid plagiarism or infringement. However, engineers may face dilemmas when presented with opportunities to use open-source code or reverse engineer proprietary software. Navigating these situations requires a deep understanding of licensing agreements, patents, and copyrights to ensure compliance and fairness.

The rapid pace of technological advancements often puts software engineers at the forefront of innovation. However, with innovation comes responsibility. Engineers may face ethical dilemmas when developing software that could potentially harm users, society, or the environment. For example, the deployment of artificial intelligence algorithms or autonomous systems can have unintended consequences. It is crucial for engineers to anticipate and mitigate these risks, prioritize safety, and uphold ethical standards.

Furthermore, software engineers often work in teams, collaborating with colleagues and stakeholders. This dynamic can introduce ethical dilemmas related to professional conduct and conflicts of interest. Engineers must maintain integrity, honesty, and transparency in their interactions, ensuring that decisions are made in the best interest of the project and the end-users.

To navigate these ethical dilemmas, software engineers must cultivate a strong ethical foundation. Continuous education and staying up-to-date with industry standards, regulations, and best practices are essential. Engaging in ethical discussions with peers, attending conferences, and participating in professional organizations can provide valuable insights and perspectives.

Ultimately, as software engineers, we have a responsibility to prioritize ethical considerations in our work. By being aware of potential dilemmas and proactively addressing them, we can contribute to the development of software that is beneficial, secure, and respectful of users' rights.

Responsibility towards Clients and Users

In the fast-paced world of software engineering, it is crucial for engineers to understand their responsibility towards clients and users. As professionals in the field of Information Technology, engineers play a significant role in developing, delivering, and maintaining software solutions that meet the needs and expectations of their clients and end-users.

One of the primary responsibilities of engineers towards clients is to ensure effective communication. This involves actively listening to clients, understanding their requirements, and translating them into technical specifications. Clear and frequent communication helps establish a strong working relationship, builds trust, and minimizes misunderstandings and rework. Engineers should be proactive in seeking feedback from clients throughout the development process to ensure that the end product aligns with their vision and goals.

Engineers also bear the responsibility of developing software solutions that are user-friendly, efficient, and reliable. They must prioritize the needs and experiences of end-users, considering factors such as usability, accessibility, and performance. This includes conducting thorough user research and testing to identify potential issues and make necessary improvements. By putting themselves in the users' shoes, engineers can create solutions that solve real problems and enhance the overall user experience.

Furthermore, engineers must ensure the security and privacy of client and user data. With the increasing number of cyber threats, it is essential to design and implement robust security measures to protect sensitive information. This involves staying updated with the latest security practices, conducting regular security audits, and addressing any vulnerabilities promptly. By prioritizing data protection, engineers can instill confidence in clients and users, safeguarding their trust and reputation.

In addition to technical responsibilities, engineers should also exhibit professionalism and ethical conduct towards clients and users. This includes respecting confidentiality agreements, providing honest and transparent information, and avoiding conflicts of interest. Engineers should strive to deliver projects on time and within budget, managing expectations and communicating any challenges or delays promptly.

Ultimately, mastering the responsibility towards clients and users is crucial for engineers in the field of software engineering. By actively engaging with clients, prioritizing user needs, ensuring security and privacy, and maintaining professionalism, engineers can deliver high-quality software solutions that meet the demands of the ever-evolving Information Technology industry.

Intellectual Property Rights

In the fast-paced and ever-evolving field of Information Technology, engineers play a crucial role in developing innovative software solutions. As engineers, we must not only be proficient in coding and programming languages but also be aware of the legal frameworks surrounding software development. This subchapter on Intellectual Property Rights aims to provide engineers in the Information Technology niche with a comprehensive understanding of the importance of protecting intellectual property and the mechanisms available for safeguarding their innovative work.

Intellectual property refers to creations of the mind, such as inventions, designs, and artistic works, that are protected by law. In the context of software engineering, intellectual property rights are vital as they ensure that the creators' innovations are legally recognized and protected from unauthorized use or replication. Understanding the various types of intellectual property rights is crucial for engineers to navigate the legal landscape effectively.

This subchapter will delve into the three main types of intellectual property rights applicable to software engineering: copyrights, patents, and trademarks. We will explore each type in detail, discussing their scope, application, and the process of obtaining protection. Additionally, we will highlight the differences between open-source software and proprietary software, emphasizing the need for engineers to be aware of potential legal pitfalls and licensing considerations.

Furthermore, this subchapter will address the importance of intellectual property rights for engineers in the context of employment. We will discuss the significance of non-disclosure agreements (NDAs) and employment contracts in protecting both the engineers and the companies they work for. Understanding the legal implications of intellectual property rights in the workplace is vital for engineers to ensure that their innovative contributions are appropriately acknowledged and protected.

Lastly, we will touch upon the ethical considerations surrounding intellectual property rights. Engineers have a responsibility to respect the intellectual property of others and avoid infringing upon existing patents or copyrights. By understanding the legal frameworks and ethical guidelines, engineers can contribute to a culture of innovation while respecting the rights of others.

In conclusion, this subchapter on Intellectual Property Rights is designed to equip engineers in the Information Technology niche with a comprehensive understanding of the legal and ethical aspects of protecting intellectual property. By mastering these concepts, engineers can confidently develop innovative software solutions while safeguarding their intellectual property and respecting the rights of others.

Professional Development and Continuing Education

In the rapidly evolving field of Information Technology, staying updated with the latest tools, techniques, and trends is crucial for engineers. Professional development and continuing education play a significant role in ensuring that engineers remain at the forefront of their industry. This subchapter explores the importance of ongoing learning and the various avenues available for engineers to enhance their skills.

In today's dynamic software engineering landscape, technologies and methodologies are constantly evolving. Engineers need to adapt to these changes to remain competitive and deliver high-quality solutions. Professional development provides engineers with the opportunity to learn new technologies, frameworks, and programming languages that are in high demand. By keeping pace with advancements, engineers can expand their skill set and increase their value in the job market.

Continuing education is not limited to technical skills alone. It also encompasses soft skills such as project management, communication, and leadership. These skills are essential for engineers to effectively collaborate with cross-functional teams and lead successful projects. Through continuing education, engineers can develop a well-rounded skill set that enables them to excel in their careers.

There are numerous avenues available for engineers to pursue professional development and continuing education. Online platforms, such as Coursera, Udemy, and LinkedIn Learning, offer a wide range of courses and certifications that cater to different skill levels and interests. These platforms provide flexibility, allowing engineers to learn at their own pace and from the comfort of their own homes. Additionally, professional organizations and industry conferences offer networking opportunities and workshops that facilitate knowledge exchange and skill development.

Employers also play a crucial role in supporting professional development and continuing education for their engineers. Organizations can provide resources, such as access to training programs and workshops, mentorship opportunities, and financial assistance for certifications. By investing in the growth and development of their engineers, companies foster a culture of continuous learning and innovation.

In conclusion, professional development and continuing education are vital for engineers in the field of Information Technology. By actively seeking opportunities to enhance their skills and knowledge, engineers can stay ahead of the curve and remain valuable assets to their organizations. From technical advancements to soft skills, ongoing learning empowers engineers to adapt to changes, tackle complex challenges, and achieve professional excellence.

Chapter 10: Emerging Trends in Software Engineering

Artificial Intelligence and Machine Learning in Software Engineering

In recent years, the fields of Artificial Intelligence (AI) and Machine Learning (ML) have rapidly gained momentum, revolutionizing various industries, including software engineering. The integration of AI and ML techniques in software engineering has opened up new possibilities and presented engineers with unprecedented opportunities to develop intelligent software systems. This subchapter delves into the fascinating world of AI and ML in software engineering, exploring their applications, benefits, and challenges.

AI and ML have emerged as powerful tools in software engineering, enabling engineers to automate complex tasks, improve software quality, and enhance overall productivity. These technologies can be used to streamline software development processes, optimize code, and make intelligent predictions. By leveraging AI and ML algorithms, engineers can improve the accuracy of software testing, detect bugs and vulnerabilities, and optimize the performance of software systems.

One of the key applications of AI and ML in software engineering is in the field of automated software development. Engineers can use AI and ML techniques to generate code, design software architectures, and automatically adapt software systems based on changing requirements. This not only speeds up the development process but also reduces the chances of human errors and improves the efficiency of software engineering teams.

Furthermore, AI and ML can be applied to improve software maintenance and support. By analyzing large amounts of historical data, AI models can predict and prevent potential software failures, enabling engineers to proactively address issues before they impact users. Additionally, ML algorithms can be trained to automatically classify and prioritize software bug reports, saving engineers valuable time and effort in the debugging process.

However, as with any emerging technology, AI and ML in software engineering also come with their own set of challenges. Ensuring the ethical use of AI and ML algorithms, addressing bias in training data, and maintaining transparency in decision-making processes are some of the key concerns that engineers need to address. Moreover, there is a need for continuous learning and upskilling to keep up with the rapid advancements in AI and ML technologies.

In conclusion, the integration of AI and ML in software engineering holds immense potential for the information technology industry. By leveraging these technologies, engineers can develop intelligent software systems that are more efficient, reliable, and adaptable. However, it is crucial for engineers to stay updated with the latest advancements, address ethical concerns, and continuously enhance their skills to harness the true power of AI and ML in software engineering.

Internet of Things (IoT) and Software Engineering

The Internet of Things (IoT) has revolutionized the way we interact with technology and the world around us. It has opened up a world of possibilities, enabling devices and objects to communicate and interact with each other through the internet. This subchapter delves into the relationship between IoT and software engineering, highlighting the crucial role software engineers play in leveraging the potential of IoT.

In the field of Information Technology, IoT has emerged as a game-changer, transforming various industries, including healthcare, manufacturing, transportation, and agriculture. As engineers in this niche, it is essential to understand the convergence of IoT and software engineering to harness its benefits fully.

Software engineering forms the backbone of IoT systems. It involves designing, developing, and maintaining the software that powers IoT devices, networks, and applications. Engineers in this field are responsible for ensuring the reliability, security, and scalability of IoT software solutions.

One of the key challenges faced by software engineers in IoT is the sheer volume and complexity of data generated by connected devices. IoT systems generate an enormous amount of data that needs to be processed, analyzed, and acted upon in real-time. Software engineers need to design and develop scalable software architectures that can handle this data efficiently.

Security is another critical aspect that software engineers must address in IoT systems. With billions of interconnected devices, the risk of cyber-attacks and data breaches is higher than ever. Engineers need to implement robust security measures, including encryption, authentication, and access control, to safeguard IoT systems from malicious actors.

Moreover, software engineers must consider the interoperability of IoT devices and platforms. As IoT ecosystems consist of diverse devices from different manufacturers, software engineers need to develop software solutions that can seamlessly integrate and communicate with these devices.

In this subchapter, we will explore various software engineering practices and techniques specific to IoT. We will discuss the importance of agile development methodologies, continuous integration, and testing in IoT projects. Additionally, we will delve into the role of cloud computing and edge computing in supporting IoT applications.

By understanding the relationship between IoT and software engineering, engineers in the field of Information Technology can unlock the full potential of this transformative technology. Mastering the art of developing scalable, secure, and interoperable software solutions for IoT will enable engineers to create innovative products and services that enhance our daily lives and drive digital transformation across industries.

DevOps and Continuous Deployment

In today's rapidly evolving digital landscape, it is becoming increasingly essential for engineers in the field of Information Technology (IT) to understand and implement DevOps and Continuous Deployment practices. These methodologies have gained significant traction in recent years due to their ability to streamline the software development and deployment processes, leading to faster delivery, improved quality, and increased customer satisfaction.

DevOps, a portmanteau of Development and Operations, is a collaborative approach that emphasizes communication, integration, and automation between software developers and IT operations professionals. By aligning these two traditionally separate teams, DevOps aims to break down silos and foster a culture of collaboration and shared responsibility.

Continuous Deployment, on the other hand, is a software engineering practice that enables frequent and automated releases of software into production. This approach emphasizes the importance of delivering small, incremental changes to production quickly and continuously, rather than waiting for large, monolithic releases. Continuous Deployment is facilitated by a robust suite of automated tests, infrastructure as code, and deployment pipelines that ensure the smooth and efficient delivery of software updates.

Engineers working in the IT industry can greatly benefit from adopting DevOps and Continuous Deployment practices. By implementing these methodologies, they can significantly reduce the time it takes to go from code commit to production deployment, resulting in faster feedback loops and accelerated time to market. Additionally, the automation and standardization inherent in these practices can greatly improve the reliability, scalability, and maintainability of software systems.

However, successfully implementing DevOps and Continuous Deployment requires a deep understanding of the underlying principles, tools, and best practices. Engineers must be well-versed in version control systems, continuous integration tools, infrastructure management, and monitoring and observability practices.

In this subchapter, "DevOps and Continuous Deployment," we will explore the fundamental concepts and techniques behind these methodologies. We will delve into the benefits and challenges of adopting DevOps and Continuous Deployment in the IT industry. Furthermore, we will provide practical guidance and real-world examples to help engineers master the art of implementing and optimizing these practices.

Whether you are a seasoned engineer looking to enhance your software engineering skills or a novice seeking to understand the latest trends in IT, this subchapter will serve as a comprehensive guide to DevOps and Continuous Deployment. By the end of this chapter, you will have the knowledge and tools necessary to transform your software development and deployment processes, ultimately contributing to the success of your organization in the ever-advancing digital landscape.

Blockchain Technology for Software Engineering

In recent years, blockchain technology has gained significant attention and emerged as a revolutionary tool in various industries, including software engineering. This subchapter will delve into the applications, benefits, and challenges of integrating blockchain technology into software engineering processes, specifically addressing engineers working in the field of information technology.

Blockchain, often associated with cryptocurrencies like Bitcoin, is a decentralized and distributed ledger technology that offers secure, transparent, and immutable records of transactions. However, its potential extends far beyond the financial realm. By leveraging blockchain technology, software engineers can enhance the development, deployment, and maintenance of software systems.

One of the primary applications of blockchain technology in software engineering is in the realm of smart contracts. Smart contracts are self-executing contracts with predefined rules and conditions. By utilizing blockchain, engineers can ensure the integrity and transparency of these contracts, eliminating the need for intermediaries and reducing the risk of fraud or tampering.

Additionally, blockchain technology provides robust security measures for software systems. Its decentralized nature makes it highly resistant to data manipulation and unauthorized access. Engineers can leverage blockchain to enhance the security of critical software components, such as authentication systems, data storage, and access controls.

Moreover, blockchain technology enables efficient and reliable software version control. Traditional version control systems often rely on a central repository, which can be vulnerable to data loss or corruption. By utilizing blockchain, engineers can create a decentralized version control system, ensuring the integrity and availability of software versions throughout the development lifecycle.

While the integration of blockchain technology into software engineering offers numerous benefits, it also presents certain challenges. Scalability remains a significant concern, as blockchain networks can become slow and inefficient when handling a large volume of transactions. Engineers must address this challenge by implementing innovative solutions, such as sharding or off-chain transactions, to ensure optimal performance.

Furthermore, the consensus mechanism used in blockchain networks, such as proof-of-work or proof-of-stake, can introduce additional complexities in software engineering processes. Engineers need to understand these mechanisms and design software systems that align with the chosen consensus algorithm.

In conclusion, blockchain technology holds immense potential for software engineering in the field of information technology. By leveraging its decentralized and secure nature, engineers can enhance the development, security, and version control of software systems. However, they must also tackle challenges related to scalability and consensus mechanisms. By mastering the integration of blockchain technology, engineers can revolutionize the software engineering landscape and pave the way for a more transparent, secure, and efficient future.

Chapter 11: Case Studies in Software Engineering

Real-life Examples of Successful Software Engineering Projects

In the fast-paced world of information technology, software engineering projects play a crucial role in shaping the way we live and work. From developing cutting-edge mobile applications to designing complex enterprise systems, software engineers are at the forefront of innovation. To gain insights into the world of successful software engineering projects, let's delve into a few real-life examples that demonstrate the power of this field.

1. The Apollo 11 Moon Landing: One of the most remarkable achievements in the history of software engineering is the Apollo 11 mission, which successfully landed humans on the moon. The software used to control the Lunar Module's guidance computer was critical to the mission's success. Developed by a team led by Margaret Hamilton, this software ensured precise navigation and enabled the astronauts to land safely on the lunar surface.

2. Google Search Engine: The Google search engine has revolutionized the way we access information. Behind its simple and intuitive interface lies a complex software engineering project that analyzes billions of web pages in real-time. The development of Google's search algorithms and infrastructure required intricate software engineering techniques to deliver accurate and relevant search results.

3. Tesla Autopilot: The Tesla Autopilot system is a prime example of how software engineering has reshaped the automotive industry. This advanced driver-assistance system utilizes machine learning and

computer vision algorithms to enable semi-autonomous driving. Through continuous software updates, Tesla improves the system's performance, making driving safer and more efficient.

4. Electronic Health Records: The implementation of electronic health records (EHR) has transformed the healthcare sector. Software engineers have developed comprehensive EHR systems that improve patient care, streamline clinical workflows, and ensure data security. These systems facilitate efficient communication among healthcare professionals, leading to better diagnosis and treatment outcomes.

5. Online Shopping Platforms: E-commerce platforms like Amazon and Alibaba have transformed the retail industry. Behind these platforms, sophisticated software engineering projects handle millions of transactions, manage inventories, and personalize customer experiences. Through data analysis and machine learning, these systems offer personalized recommendations and optimize supply chain management.

These real-life examples highlight the diverse applications of software engineering in various industries. From space exploration to healthcare and e-commerce, engineers in the field of information technology have the power to shape the world we live in. By mastering software engineering techniques and staying abreast of the latest advancements, engineers can continue to develop innovative solutions that drive progress and improve our lives.

Lessons Learned from Failed Software Projects

In the fast-paced world of Information Technology, software projects often fail to live up to expectations. Whether it's a lack of proper planning, miscommunication, or inadequate testing, these failures can have a significant impact on an organization's resources, reputation, and bottom line. However, as engineers, it is crucial to learn from these failures and implement strategies to avoid them in future projects. This subchapter titled "Lessons Learned from Failed Software Projects" in the book "Mastering Software Engineering: A Comprehensive Guide for Engineers" aims to equip engineers in the field of Information Technology with the necessary insights to overcome common pitfalls.

One of the key lessons to take away from failed software projects is the importance of proper planning and requirements gathering. Rushing into a project without a clear understanding of client needs and objectives can lead to scope creep, missed deadlines, and unsatisfied stakeholders. Engineers must learn to invest time in thorough analysis and documentation of requirements to ensure that the project's goals are well-defined and achievable.

Another critical lesson is the significance of effective communication within the project team and with stakeholders. Many software projects fail due to miscommunication between developers, designers, testers, and project managers. Engineers must learn to communicate effectively, articulate their ideas clearly, and actively listen to others. Regular team meetings, progress updates, and feedback sessions can help minimize misunderstandings and keep everyone on the same page.

Testing and quality assurance play a crucial role in the success of software projects. Neglecting or rushing through these phases can lead to software with numerous bugs and vulnerabilities. Engineers must prioritize comprehensive testing at every stage of development and invest in robust quality assurance processes. Implementing automated testing tools and conducting thorough code reviews can help identify and rectify issues before they become major roadblocks.

Lastly, engineers must be adaptable and responsive to change. Technology and client requirements are constantly evolving, and projects that fail to adapt to these changes are more likely to fail. Embracing agile methodologies, such as Scrum or Kanban, can help teams quickly respond to changing requirements and deliver value incrementally.

In conclusion, failed software projects provide invaluable lessons for engineers in the field of Information Technology. By learning from past mistakes, engineers can improve their planning, communication, testing, and adaptability skills. This subchapter aims to equip engineers with the knowledge and strategies to navigate future software projects successfully, ultimately ensuring the satisfaction of stakeholders and the continued growth of the organization.

Best Practices and Success Factors in Software Engineering

In the rapidly evolving field of software engineering, mastering best practices and understanding success factors is essential for engineers to excel in their careers. This subchapter delves into the key principles and strategies that are crucial for success in the information technology niche.

1. Agile Methodologies: Embracing agile methodologies has become a cornerstone of successful software engineering. Engineers must understand and implement practices such as Scrum and Kanban, enabling them to deliver high-quality software in short iterations. Agile methodologies prioritize collaboration, adaptability, and continuous improvement, allowing engineers to respond effectively to changing requirements.

2. Code Quality and Testing: Writing clean, maintainable code is fundamental to software engineering excellence. Engineers must adhere to industry best practices, such as following coding standards and performing thorough unit testing. By incorporating code reviews and leveraging automated testing frameworks, engineers can identify and rectify potential issues early in the development process, ensuring robust and reliable software.

3. Continuous Integration and Deployment: Streamlining the software development lifecycle through continuous integration and deployment practices is vital. Engineers should adopt tools and practices that automate the build, test, and deployment processes, enabling frequent releases and reducing manual errors. This approach enhances

collaboration, accelerates time to market, and improves overall software quality.

4. Documentation and Communication: Effective communication and comprehensive documentation are critical for successful software engineering. Engineers must be proficient in expressing ideas clearly, both verbally and in writing, to collaborate effectively with team members and stakeholders. Additionally, maintaining up-to-date documentation ensures knowledge transfer and ease of maintenance for future development.

5. Project Management and Collaboration: Software engineering projects often involve multiple stakeholders and team members. Engineers should familiarize themselves with project management methodologies, such as Agile or Waterfall, to effectively plan, track, and deliver projects on time and within budget. Collaborative tools and practices, such as version control systems and project management software, facilitate seamless teamwork and enhance productivity.

6. Continuous Learning and Professional Development: The field of software engineering is ever-evolving, requiring engineers to stay abreast of emerging technologies and industry trends. Continuous learning through attending conferences, workshops, and online courses enables engineers to acquire new skills and enhance their expertise. Engaging in professional development activities not only benefits individual engineers but also contributes to the growth and success of the organization.

By embracing these best practices and success factors in software engineering, engineers in the information technology niche can elevate their skills, contribute to high-quality software, and drive innovation in their organizations. Mastering these principles is a continuous journey that ensures engineers remain at the forefront of the dynamic field of software engineering.

Chapter 12: Conclusion

Recap of Key Concepts

As engineers in the field of Information Technology, it is crucial to have a solid understanding of the key concepts that underpin the practice of software engineering. In this subchapter, we will provide a recap of these fundamental concepts, ensuring that you have a firm grasp on the principles that govern this discipline.

One of the most important concepts in software engineering is the software development life cycle (SDLC). This encompasses the entire process of developing software, starting from requirements gathering and analysis, through design, coding, testing, and deployment. Understanding the different phases of the SDLC and their interdependencies is vital for successfully delivering high-quality software projects.

Another critical concept is the importance of maintaining code quality. Well-structured, modular, and maintainable code is the backbone of any successful software project. Engineers must be aware of best practices in code organization, documentation, and testing to ensure that software is robust, scalable, and easy to maintain over time.

Additionally, software engineers must have a solid understanding of various software design patterns. These patterns provide proven solutions to common design problems and promote software that is reusable, extensible, and loosely coupled. By understanding and applying these patterns, engineers can create software that is not only efficient but also easy to understand and modify.

Version control is another concept that engineers must master. Version control systems allow teams to collaborate effectively, track changes, and manage different versions of their codebase. By utilizing version control tools, engineers can avoid conflicts, rollback to previous versions if necessary, and ensure the stability and integrity of their software projects.

Lastly, software engineers must always consider the importance of security in their work. With the increasing number of cyber threats, engineers need to be aware of best practices for secure coding, data encryption, and vulnerability testing. By implementing robust security measures, engineers can protect sensitive data and ensure the safety and reliability of their software systems.

In conclusion, this subchapter has provided a recap of key concepts in software engineering, aiming to reinforce the understanding of engineers in the field of Information Technology. By mastering these concepts, engineers can enhance their ability to develop high-quality software, effectively collaborate with teams, and create secure and reliable software systems.

Future Directions in Software Engineering

As engineers working in the field of Information Technology, it is essential to stay updated with the latest trends and future directions in software engineering. The field of software engineering is constantly evolving, driven by technological advancements and changing user demands. In this subchapter, we will explore some of the future directions that software engineering is expected to take.

1. Artificial Intelligence and Machine Learning: AI and ML have already made significant impacts in various industries, and the software engineering field is no exception. In the future, we can expect software engineers to leverage AI and ML techniques to develop intelligent software systems that can automate complex tasks, improve decision-making processes, and enhance user experiences.

2. Internet of Things (IoT): The IoT has revolutionized the way we interact with technology, with interconnected devices becoming increasingly common. Software engineers will play a crucial role in developing robust and secure software systems to support the growing IoT ecosystem. This includes designing efficient communication protocols, ensuring data privacy and security, and developing scalable software architectures.

3. DevOps and Agile Development: DevOps and Agile methodologies have gained widespread adoption in recent years, enabling faster and more efficient software development and deployment. Future software engineers will need to master these methodologies, as they continue to evolve and become integral parts of software development processes.

4. Cybersecurity: With the increasing reliance on software systems and the growing number of cyber threats, cybersecurity has become a top priority. Software engineers will need to focus on developing secure software systems, implementing robust authentication and encryption mechanisms, and staying updated with the latest security protocols and practices.

5. Cloud Computing: Cloud computing has transformed the way software is developed, deployed, and managed. Software engineers will need to adapt to the cloud-centric paradigm and develop skills in cloud computing technologies such as virtualization, containerization, and serverless computing.

6. User Experience (UX) Design: User experience has become a key differentiator in software products and services. Software engineers will need to collaborate closely with UX designers to develop software systems that provide intuitive interfaces, seamless interactions, and personalized experiences.

7. Big Data and Analytics: The exponential growth of data has created a need for software engineers skilled in big data processing and analytics. Future software engineers will need to develop expertise in handling and analyzing large datasets to derive meaningful insights and support data-driven decision making.

In conclusion, the future of software engineering holds exciting opportunities and challenges. As engineers in the field of Information Technology, it is crucial to stay updated with the latest trends and continually upgrade our skills to adapt to the evolving landscape. By embracing emerging technologies and methodologies, software engineers can play a significant role in shaping the future of software engineering and driving innovation in the IT industry.

Final Thoughts and Recommendations for Engineers

As we conclude this comprehensive guide on mastering software engineering, it is important to highlight some final thoughts and provide recommendations specifically tailored to engineers working in the field of information technology. These insights will help you navigate the dynamic and ever-evolving world of software engineering with confidence and expertise.

Firstly, it is crucial to embrace a growth mindset. The field of information technology is constantly changing, with new technologies, frameworks, and tools emerging regularly. To stay ahead, engineers must adopt a mindset that encourages continuous learning and improvement. Embrace opportunities to update your skills, stay current with industry trends, and explore new technologies. This will not only enhance your professional growth but also make you a valuable asset to any organization.

Secondly, collaboration is key. In the world of software engineering, teamwork and effective communication are essential. Seek opportunities to work with other engineers, participate in group projects, and engage in discussions within your professional community. This will not only broaden your perspective but also expose you to different approaches and solutions that can significantly enhance your own problem-solving skills.

Thirdly, prioritize quality and maintainability in your software development process. As an engineer, it is your responsibility to produce software that is reliable, efficient, and maintainable. Write clean and well-documented code, follow best practices, and invest time in testing and debugging. By doing so, you will not only deliver high-quality products but also reduce the chances of bugs and technical debt, ultimately saving time and effort in the long run.

Additionally, never underestimate the importance of soft skills. While technical expertise is essential, effective communication, leadership, and teamwork skills are equally valuable. As an engineer, you will often collaborate with cross-functional teams, interact with clients, and communicate complex ideas to non-technical stakeholders. Sharpening these soft skills will enable you to effectively communicate your ideas, build strong relationships, and advance in your career.

Lastly, never stop networking and building relationships within the industry. Attend conferences, join professional organizations, and engage in online communities. Networking not only opens doors to new opportunities but also allows you to learn from experienced professionals and gain insights into the latest trends and advancements in the field of software engineering.

In conclusion, as an engineer in the information technology niche, mastering software engineering requires a growth mindset, collaboration, a focus on quality, soft skills, and an active presence in the industry. By implementing these final thoughts and recommendations, you will be well-equipped to excel in your career and contribute meaningfully to the ever-evolving world of software engineering.

www.ingramcontent.com/pod-product-compliance
Lightning Source LLC
LaVergne TN
LVHW051956060526
838201LV00059B/3678